FROM TRAUMA TO TRIUMPH

Edited by Little Blk Books, LLC
Cover design by Raiona Denise Enterprise
Cover photo by Fond Memories Photography

Published by Brown & Brown Publishing
68 Watkins Dr. #4231
Upper Marlboro, MD 20774

bbpublishinghelp@gmail.com

Printed in the United States of America.

FROM TRAUMA TO TRIUMPH

Healing the Unspoken Wounds

TAMEKA SHELONE

BROWN & BROWN

PUBLISHING

CONTENTS

Introduction   *ix*

PART I

MY TRAUMA, MY TRUTH

1 WHERE IT ALL BEGAN   3

2 BREAKING THE SILENCE   11

3 BEHIND THE MASK   25

PART II

ROADMAP TO HEALING AND RECOVERY

4 LET THE HEALING BEGIN   39

5 FACE YOUR TRUTH   51

   Reflection   56

6 FEEL WHAT YOU FEEL   59

   Reflection   64

7 FORGIVE AND FORGET   67

   Reflection   73

PART III

GREAT VICTORY!

8 BE FREE AND MOVE FORWARD   79

CONCLUSION   87

   Resources   *88*

   End Notes   *89*

   Acknowledgments   *90*

   Stay Connected   *93*

   About The Author   *94*

   Reflection   *96*

DEDICATION

*I dedicate this book to the One who breathed life into me and reminded me that I was born with a purpose greater than my pain. **God**, thank you for giving me the strength and courage to tell my story so that others may be healed and set free.*

*To my angel in heaven, **Rosolyn M. Brown**, an amazing writer and poet with such a creative mind, this one's for you. Although you left this earth before publishing your work, your legacy continues. This body of work is dedicated to you, my cousin and friend.*

INTRODUCTION

Life has a way of happening to the best of us. Often it brings out the worse in us. I vividly remember the dark nights of despair, the days of doom and gloom, and the secrets of my soul that crushed me deeply. Those secrets caused me to hide in the shadows of my own wings. Finding it difficult to truly soar when haunted by the memories of my past, I often crawled into a fetal position, rocking myself to sleep, hoping to be awakened from the nightmare that was my reality.

From the outside, I was well put together, educated, and successful. I served in ministry and the community. I was preaching, praying, and prophesying. I traveled the world and had a good time. And all these things were in fact my reality. But so was the hurt, pain, and brokenness. Being guarded, defensive, confused, and simply put, a wounded woman, I tried to figure out what in the world was wrong with me. Have you ever been there? On one hand all seems to be grand, but on the other, internally and emotionally, you're a wreck!

After a couple of years in the forty and over club, successful and single again, I paused and began to do some personal reflection; I sought some truths about my reality. I needed to do a deep dive into relationships. Not just romantic relationships, but *all* relationships. And there lay the beginning of some deep-rooted issues that surfaced and led me to begin my healing journey. It was through prayer, professional help, and journaling that I was able to get to the root of the matter: trauma. The hidden and unspoken wounds were slowly but surely being uncovered, one layer at a time. It's the unspoken wound that is the unattended wound, and the unattended wound is the unhealed wound. One thing I discovered is if you want to get to the truth of the matter, you have to get to the root of the matter. Now I must admit, when I discovered that I had experienced "trauma," I sought immediate attention in the form of therapy. I never thought of any of my experiences as "traumatic." That word seemed so harsh and unbefitting to the image I was trying to uphold. I was in denial of the pain and its affects. I suppressed every emotion and became numb to how trauma made me feel. But in actuality, I had been traumatized by the experiences that I tried to ignore. Keep reading, and I'll unpack that for you.

If you want to get to the truth of the matter, you have to get to the root of the matter.

According to Integratedlistening.com, "Trauma is the response to a deeply distressing or disturbing event that overwhelms an individual's ability to cope, causes feelings of helplessness, diminishes their sense of self and their ability to feel the full range of emotions and experiences."[i] Trauma is a result of various experiences and events in life. Some of those events that cause trauma include violence, poverty, abuse, rape, molestation, abortion, adultery, divorce, war, death, untimely accidents and incidents, and other tragic events. If you can identify with any of these events and have found it difficult to feel the emotions associated with the experiences and process them fully, it could be that it is just too traumatic for you to handle. As a result, you suppress the emotions and avoid dealing with the effects of the event; sometimes pretending that it didn't happen or telling yourself it is what it is.

Have you ever experienced life in such a way that it left you numb? The kind of experience that you prefer not to talk about or deal with? The ones that left you feeling sad, depressed, ashamed, embarrassed, guilty, or even tainted? Or what about emotionally detached, mentally drained, physically depleted, spiritually wounded? I, too, have had some of those experiences. And the truth of the matter is sometimes these experiences and the emotions attached to them are inescapable. You think you have escaped them because you've buried them. In reality, they are lying dormant and will rear their ugly head when you least expect it. It shows up in how you react when you are triggered by the memories of the experience. It even shows up in who you choose to attach yourself to.

The traumatic experiences and events of our lives have the propensity to alter the very essence of who we are at our core. These experiences and events affect us emotionally, physically, psychologically, and even spiritually. Trauma has knocked on many of our doors uninvited, and instead of welcoming it in, it forcibly entered and left many of us broken, bruised, and bound. The good news is that it does not have to stay. No matter how long trauma has taken up residence, now is a good time to serve its eviction notice and begin the work to heal, be free, and to be made whole.

As a trained counselor, certified trauma support specialist, mental health advocate, and certified professional life coach, my passion for helping women heal and recover a healthy sense of self is my purpose. While I do not write from the lens of a psychologist or therapist, I do share my experiences, educational knowledge, wisdom, godly principles and promises as a result of putting in hard work to manifest healing and wholeness in my life.

Throughout the book, you will see "pause breaks." This is an opportunity for you to journal your emotions through simple, targeted writing prompts. As I share my story, I'm aware that many of you may become triggered by the memories of your own experience. I want to ensure that I offer a moment for you to ground yourself before going any further. Self-regulation is an important tool when your emotions are triggered. Here are a few suggestions for you: take a sip of water, practice breathing techniques, take a walk and practice mindfulness meditation. Mindfulness meditation is being present and allowing yourself to feel everything as is, without judgment. You'll also be provided space to reflect and journal your thoughts. Don't bottle your emotions; free them by documenting them in the blank pages provided for you. Revelation 12:11 reminds us that we overcome "by the blood of the Lamb and the word of their testimony." (Revelation 12:11 NIV) It is my hope that the words of my testimony will help you overcome your trauma and heal the wounds of your past.

As you flip through the pages of my life, I urge you to pause and breath slowly, reflect over your own life, and apply the tools and strategies provided to begin your personal healing journey. Nobody said the road would be easy, but I don't believe you've come this far to be defeated. Victory, healing, and wholeness are yours. Healing is not just for me. It's available to you, too. Let me help you shift from trauma to triumph!

PART I

MY TRAUMA, MY TRUTH

"Trauma is not what happens to you. Trauma is what happens inside you as a result of what happens to you." - Gabor Maté

WHERE IT ALL BEGAN

In the beginning…

The exposure to trauma often happens during our formative years. However, the symptoms usually don't appear until later in our adult years. As a child born in Washington, DC, and reared in South Carolina for eleven years before returning to the DMV (DC, Maryland, Virginia area), I was raised by my mother as an only child. I remember the little girl who was stuck like glue to her mamma's side. Riding through town with her hand hanging out the window bopping to some of the 70's hits or posing for pictures with that same hand on her hips—just grown! Whenever you saw Ms. Brown, you saw me. Except for the times she went out to get her two-step on, dancing is what we both LOVED. I couldn't go but would chase down the car like a wild woman, crying and screaming furiously while she sped off down those dark, pitch-black country roads. Don't worry, she never left me out there alone. Either one of my aunts would come get me or she would stop, turn around, put me in the car, and take me back to the house. Talk about attachment issues and a mamma's girl! My mother made sure all of my needs were met. She provided a safe place for me to lay my head, ensuring I had the necessities of life and many of the things I desired.

Can we talk about the outfits she made for me and how we dressed alike and flicked it up in pictures? The beautiful dresses and hair bows, lace socks and patent leather shoes —if you're wondering where I get my love of clothes and the camera from, now you know. Oh, the memories! Mom gave me the emotional support I needed and made sure the foundation of faith was instilled in me. She showered me with her love, not only telling me that she loved me daily, but showed me just how much she did. Singing loudly, "I'll always love my mamma, she's my favorite girl —you only get one, you only get one, yeah!"

A mother-daughter relationship is such a beautiful thing. I appreciate all the memories and good times I shared with my mom and continue to share even to this day. However, there's another relationship that is just as important to little girls. The father-daughter relationship. This relationship plays a pivotal role in shaping how girls view themselves and what they believe about themselves. It also shows what future male relationships and interactions would look like. A father's presence or absence, physically and emotionally, is a reflection of a daughter's self-image, value, worth, and perception of men, negatively and positively. The little girl longs to hear daddy's voice and to have him near to show up and support her during all her most important moments. Now, for some of you, you may have grown up in homes absent of your biological mother and/or father, which was totally out of your control. You may have been raised by other caregivers such as grandparents, bonus parents, foster parents, adoptive parents, godparents or others who took on the responsibility of caring and providing for you. You may not have had your biological parent, but the presence or absence of that maternal or paternal figure, has certainly had some effect on who you are today.

While my father did not raise me and was not fully present most of my life, I knew exactly who he was. In fact, I have memories of him. This charismatic man had a way of saying "baby" whenever I saw him or spoke with him. He said it with a strong southern accent and smooth tone that my face would light up and I would have the biggest smile. You couldn't tell me I wasn't his baby. Hearing that one word made me feel so loved and protected. As a little girl, I recall the brief moments we would spend together when he stopped by the house or came by to scoop me up for a ride through town. I remember going to his mom's house and she always had a peach soda stashed away in the closet just for me. These moments were few and far between, oh, but I remember. You'll notice that there aren't nearly as many memories as those shared with my mom. But there was this one I do recall. I was maybe six or seven years old. He dropped me off after taking me for a ride through town. The town with one traffic light, one grocery store; the town where everybody knew everybody. I remember him saying something to the tune of I'll see you soon —soon like the next day, soon like later in the week, the weekend? Needless to say, soon never came. If my memory serves me correctly, and I think it does, I never physically saw him again. However, as time went on and I grew older, I would have very brief conversations with him by phone.

Can you imagine a little girl standing in a chair looking out the window as Daddy drove off, awaiting the next time he would come by? As days, weeks, years go by, she's still staring out the window. This, my loves, was the root of my first case of trauma: abandonment. Just like that, he disappears into the night and the days of longing to see him and to know him became long and endless. As a child, I didn't know that "abandonment trauma" was a thing and certainly didn't know the impact it would have on me as a teen or adult.

When a parent is absent in a child's life, physical and emotional needs are unmet and cause unhealthy human development. It doesn't matter if it's the absence of a mother or father; in my case, it was my father. The symptoms and impact of the abandonment did not show up until my later teens and adulthood. It began to rear its ugly head in unhealthy relationship choices, seeking safety and validation from men to fill a void, and looking for love in all the wrong places. Some of the signs and symptoms included trust issues, insecurities, settling, lack of emotional depth and intimacy, and other fears. Can you relate?

While my father was no longer physically or emotionally present, he would resurface every so often and reach out to me by phone. The calls he made to me always ended with "You know I love you, right?" and as a young child, preteen, teen, and young adult, I was confused about a father's love. I recall early on responding by saying, "Yes, I know, and I love you, too." Did I really know what love was, or was this the normal call-and-response reply? I remember once returning one of his calls when I was about twenty-two years old, he ended the call as he normally does. My reply this time was different. I said, "No, I don't." He was shocked and proceeded to explain that he does love me and apologized for not being there for me. It was at this point that I could no longer accept his "I love yous" by words. I needed action. What did "I love you" look like for me up to this point? Absence, sporadic phone calls, coming around when it was convenient, just mere words with no action. The kind of "I love yous" I received from my father shaped my view of love in many of my male relationships.

I remember having a conversation with my former pastor about my biological father. There was one question he raised that I will never forget. He said, "Have you ever thought about when your father says he loves you, that he loves you from the capacity he knows love?" Whoaaah! That has stuck with me ever since and changed my perception of him and of love. You see, there's truth to that. People can only love you to the capacity they knew love. Often we try to project our way of loving, or even needing love, on others who don't have the capacity to love us in that way. We have no idea how love was shown or expressed or given to that person; yet, we expect them to just "know" how to love us. People only know what they know; not always what we "think" they should know. So, this caused me to pause and ponder thoughts of how he may have been shown love: what his relationship may or may not have been like with his parents —did he experience some of the behaviors he was exhibiting toward me (and his other children for that matter)? So many questions, but the one thing it did allow me to do was to extend him grace.

People can only love you to the capacity they knew love.

While I've come to know that my father was not in the best place or space in his life to provide the physical or emotional support I needed as his child, I'm grateful for a Father's love that has proven to be the kind of love that is consistent and everlasting. Abba Father promises never to leave us nor forsake us, but to be with us. He will never abandon us. That's His promise and one I learned to stand flat footed on while healing the father wound. God promises in Psalm 68:5 to be a "father to the fatherless."

(Psalm 68:5 NIV) When our earthly fathers are unable to take responsibility for what they produced, fret not. Out heavenly Father always comes through on His word and shows up for us.

For those of you who may have experienced trauma from the abandonment of a biological parent, know that you're not alone. Sometimes God allows us to be rejected simply to protect us. We may not have understood it then but let this be a moment of understanding now. Be aware of the symptoms and triggers of abandonment trauma.

2

BREAKING THE SILENCE

"When we find the courage to share our experiences and the compassion to hear others tell their stories, we force shame out of hiding, and end the silence." -Brené Brown

Whenever there is a physical injury, it requires immediate attention so that proper medical assistance is provided. When we have been emotionally and mentally wounded by the experiences of life, we require that same immediate attention and proper assistance. Often, these wounds are hidden, and as a result, unspoken. The thought of talking about it makes you cringe, causes your chest to tighten, your heart to race, and your eyes to water. But can I tell you that it is the hidden and unspoken wounds that are causing more damage to your emotional and mental state than you actually realize? For some, it is too painful to talk about. The family secrets, the abuse, the incest, the infidelity. The secret is killing you more than the actual experience. For others, it is safer for you to pretend it never happened and live in the lie. This spares you from being vulnerable and having to face the pain of your experience. You can't own your truth if you insist on living a lie. Releasing yourself from the shackles of lies will create a new feeling of freedom that you never knew you needed.

I will never forget the year I graduated from high school and went away to college. Well, it wasn't really *away* since my university was less than an hour from my home; however, I did stay on campus my first year. It was 1995 when I began my HBCU (Historically Black College and University) journey. My mom and stepfather dropped me off on campus, we decorated my dorm room, and all the excitement and nervousness flooded my emotional tank. Of course, I was happy to have my freedom and independence but a little nervous about the unknowns of college and campus life. I graduated from high school as an honor student and entered college a virgin. I was the good ol' "church girl" friend in the tribe who was definitely waiting until I was married to have sex, start a family, and live happily ever after. I had it all planned out —or so I thought.

I soon found myself exploring my first "relationship." He was older than me and much more experienced at this thing called life. He gave me what I was missing: protection, attention, and love. He filled the void my father left. Can I be honest and tell you

I had no idea what I was doing or what I was looking for in a relationship? And what I did know was not enough to consider myself ready to fully engage in one. I was just going with the flow.

We were a couple for several months, getting to know each other, strengthening our connection. He was keenly aware of my stance on sex before marriage and that my primary focus was getting through college. While seemingly pretty mature for my age, I'm sure he was also aware of just how emotionally immature I was. One day I went to visit him, which wasn't uncommon, especially on the weekends. I had my own car but couldn't keep it on campus so I would go home on the weekends. We were alone which wasn't uncommon. What was different was him luring me to a room that wasn't the typical location we would spend time. He began kissing and fondling me. I became highly agitated and yelled at him to STOP! After repeated *nos* and *stop*s, the unimaginable happened. At just eighteen years old, I became a date rape victim.

Inhale. Exhale. Breathe. Repeat.

I remember staring out the window watching the cars go by in disbelief, anger, disappointment, and disgrace. I kept telling myself to just breathe. I think I counted every breath. He reached over to hug me. I pushed him away. I did not want to be touched. I felt dirty. Tainted. Filthy. Disgusting. Just that quickly, my innocence was gone. Can you imagine what was going through

my mind? Actually, I couldn't think. For a moment I blanked out.
I finally got myself together, got up, and went to the bathroom. As
I wiped myself, I noticed blood. Tears fell down my face. I left
quickly, leaving a part of me in that bathroom.

You see, for me and many others who have experienced
rape at the hands of someone they know, it is hard to stomach that
they would do such a thing. For twenty-five years, I told myself it
was "unconsented sex." Well, is that not what rape is in its
simplest form? It was the hardest thing for me to say because in
my mind, I would then be a statistic, a victim. Truth is, even
without me calling it rape back then, I was already a statistic and
a victim of it. According to Merriam-Webster, rape is defined as
"unlawful sexual activity and usually sexual intercourse carried
out forcibly or under threat of injury against a person's will."[ii] It
doesn't matter if it's someone you know or not, if it was forced
and unconsented, it is rape. It is unlawful. It is traumatizing. But
you are not alone.

I recall years ago being asked to speak at a women's shut-
in at my church. I attempted to speak on the trauma of Tamar who
was raped by her brother Amnon. He plotted to sleep with her.
She cried out for him not to do such a thing. "But Amnon wouldn't
listen to her, and since he was stronger than she was, he raped her"
(2 Samuel 13:14 NLT). Can you imagine the hurt, pain, and shame
she must have felt? These are the same emotions I felt when I
experienced rape as well as when I attempted to minister the
message. When I mounted the pulpit to minister, after reading the

scripture, I immediately became nauseous and unable to stand. I remember my mother and other ladies walking me to a bench, and as I went to sit down, I vomited. After about an hour, I began to feel better and was able to finish the message. It was the craziest, most unexplainable thing that ever happened. What I didn't know then, that I've come to know now, is that my body was responding to the similarities between Tamar's trauma and mine. I had not yet dealt with my trauma in a way that I could fully deliver the message. I believe at that point God was uprooting the seed that was planted so I could begin to heal. As you can see through this biblical example, none of us are immune from deeply distressing and disturbing experiences.

Several weeks went by after the rape. I had very limited conversations with him. I needed some time to process my emotions and everything that had happened. I'm sure I didn't do a good job processing. I tried to go on with life as normal. Back in class. An emotional wreck. As the days went by, I started to feel sick. I noticed I missed my cycle. My nerves were all over the place. I knew in my gut that something was not right. I decided to take a pregnancy test, and low and behold, the results caused me to spiral. I was pregnant. My heart dropped. I felt like I had just gotten hit by an 18-wheeler. I felt like my life was over. Remember, I was the good ol' church girl waiting until marriage to have sex and start a family. What in the world was I going to do? Emotions raged even more. Confused. Alone. This was all foreign to me. I began to miss classes; unfocused and emotionally tortured. Certainly, I would not tell my mother. And I couldn't turn to the church. This couldn't get out to my family.

One of my professors became concerned about my absences and noticed that I wasn't myself. She pulled me to the side one day after class to inquire. Before I could get a word out, tears began to fall down my face. Shame overtook me, and I bowed my head and sobbed. After a few minutes, I broke through the tears and silence and told her I was pregnant. The thoughts and memories of how I became pregnant flooded my mind. She embraced me and assured me everything was going to be okay. When she hugged me, I literally fell in her arms and for the first time in weeks felt a sense of safety. I was safe to let go of all I was holding inside and dealing with alone. I spared her the details of the rape and who the person was but did tell her it was my first time having sex. She allowed me the space to be vulnerable as she listened and offered guidance and advice.

I recall us talking again about a week later and she wanted to know what I decided to do. She shared that she didn't have children and was unable to conceive. While the decision to keep or abort the baby was ultimately up to me, as an option, she did offer to adopt the baby if I decided to keep my child. Whoaaah! This added another layer of emotions. That means I would have to carry my child and then give her away to my professor? I was confused and torn between knowing the *right* thing to do and grappling with the reality of having a child out of wedlock as a result of rape. I was fighting the feelings of fear, embarrassment, shame, and even selfishness. Thinking about what other people would think or say. Thinking about how having this child would impact my life. If I would be able to finish my college degree. So many thoughts and emotions running through my mind. My professor, who became one of my mentors, was a trusted voice of reason and source of strength to help guide me personally and academically. We would check-in weekly. Our conversations made me feel safe to talk about my truth. She assured me that whatever decision I made I would be fine. I was concerned about my academic term and if I would be able to pull through after missing classes and assignments. She advised me to talk with my professors to let them know I was experiencing some personal challenges and request additional time to make up missed assignments. My requests were granted, and I was able to complete the semester with a 3.0.

The time had come when I had to make a decision. I begin researching abortions to try to understand the process and procedures. I researched places I could go if I decided to go through with an abortion. The guy I had been dating, who raped and impregnated me, already had children. After having a conversation with him about my pregnancy, he asked what I was going to do. I started to think about my future and his situation and lifestyle. I had a major decision to make. Taking all things into consideration, I decided to abort my child. I scheduled my appointment and contacted a girlfriend of mine to accompany me to the appointment as I would need someone to drive me home afterwards.

It was a fall Saturday morning in 1995 when I prepared myself to go to Planned Parenthood in Washington, DC. I was anxious and afraid. All kinds of thoughts clouded my mind. I remember heading to the front door of the abortion clinic and seeing the protestors. They were handing out pamphlets and calling us murderers. I made my way inside, signed in, and sat in the waiting room with other women there for the same reason I was. Still, I felt embarrassed and ashamed and like the biggest sinner ever. I filled out papers and was called back to get my procedure. I remember the nurse asking a series of questions, explaining the procedure, and confirming I wanted to go through with this. I confirmed. What happened next, ripped my heart open.

I remember laying on the table with my eyes closed fighting back the tears as the doctor proceeded with the abortion procedure. The nurse held my hands. Tears began to fall down my face. Thoughts raced through my head. *This could not be happening. Is God mad with me? Will I ever be forgiven? I have got to be the worse person in the world.* Once the procedure was complete, I went to the recovery room with other ladies and I sat quietly ready to run out of there and awaken from this nightmare. No, it was my reality.

Inhale. Exhale. Breathe. Repeat.

I didn't say much as my girlfriend drove me from Planned Parenthood to her house. She didn't live too far so I managed to drive myself the rest of the way home. Wouldn't you know, my mom was outside raking leaves. I was in pain. I had been crying and was ready to get in the bed. I spoke, giving little to no conversation, hurried inside, and crawled in the bed. Once I was in my bed, I broke down. Sobbing quietly enough to not alarm anyone, I took the medicine that was prescribed to me and drifted off to sleep. I awakened to the feelings of guilt, shame, and condemnation; feelings I would carry with me for twenty-five years, a secret I planned to take to my grave. The only people I told was my professor, my girlfriend, and my doctor because I had to go to him for a check-up and disclose this information.

Life quickly went back to normal. No counseling or therapy. No professional help to assist me with processing all I went through. Just life back to normal as I knew it at eighteen years old. Not only was I traumatized by the rape but grief-stricken due to aborting my unborn child. I grieved the loss of a child I never gave a chance. I remember being in church on the Sundays when babies were dedicated to God. A known Christian practice in the Baptist church is baby dedications. At my former church, parents of babies would have them dedicated, or given back to God. I would sit and cry what looked like tears of joy to everyone else. It was triggering; I would always think about the child I did not carry. Eventually, I pushed those emotions so far down that I was able to contain them during baby dedications, baby showers, and birth celebrations.

I carried the weight of my unspoken wounds for twenty-five years, never realizing just how it negatively impacted my life. I continued down a spiral of unhealthy and unsafe relationships. My value and worth were diminished. I would attach myself to men I was not emotionally available to. The "I love yous" and "you're so beautiful" and "you're so sexy" "you're so smart and have so much going for yourself" were all exchanged for sex, a few dinners, and a good time. Not a whole lot of actions, just mere words. It didn't require a commitment, just a connection. I didn't demand much; therefore, I didn't get much.

I graduated from college in 1999, began my career in education, had my own apartment, purchased a home a year or so later, had my own car, paid my own bills, and could take care of myself. I was of the mindset "I don't need no man for nothing." Because most times I didn't feel safe, I shielded myself and my emotions by not fully committing, pushing them away before they walked away, or have a fit if they decided to end it before I could. I needed to feel like I was in control to feel safe. Listen, these are all behaviors rooted in abandonment, violation, and feeling unsafe. These are behaviors that spanned over fifteen years.

One day, many years later, I went to Christian counseling. On my intake form there was a question about number of children, pregnancies, and abortions. I attempted to leave the abortion line blank but then I was convicted to enter my truth. My counselor helped me process the grief of not having my child. She prayed with me. Later when I got home, I began to pour my heart out to God about my choices and sins. The Father reminded me of two things: he would forgive me the moment I prayed and asked for forgiveness and that "therefore, there is now no condemnation for those who are in Christ Jesus, because through Christ Jesus the law of the Spirit who gives life has set you free" (Romans 8:1, 2 NIV).

It was the unspoken wound that stole my voice, kept me stuck, and continuously made me sick. I appeared fine on the outside, but in the inside, my past trauma was killing me. There was a war going on and it was time for it to end. My determination to win this battle kicked into full throttle and I began to do the work to gain my voice by breaking the silence. First, I recognized that I needed assistance. I had been living and reacting to trauma the same way for years. It's hard to break habits, so I sought out someone to help me through it. It's good to ask a trusted coach, mentor, or elder for help. In my case, I confided in her when no one else was available. What I said to her was the truth about how I lost my voice in the first place. She recommended I see a therapist. Reaching out to those who are trained to help you deal with what's causing you the most pain is an eye opening experience. Therapy allowed me to open up, be vulnerable, and feel safe with sharing my experiences. I was able to trust my therapist with my truth. I no longer felt the need to keep silent. I finally gained my voice back.

Truth is, I didn't talk about a lot of the trauma I experienced, so I thought I was healed from it. Wrong! Not talking about it only deepened the wounds. Removing the bandage and uncovering the wound is what's necessary for healing to manifest. In order to heal, we have to be willing to deal with the parts of us that we often try to ignore or mask. At some point in our lives, the residue of the experience will bleed out and propel us to deal with the root cause of our pain. It will show up in relationships, professional situations, and even family relationships. You may find yourself building a wall, which sometimes keeps the right people from coming into your life. Truth is, trauma may affect you, but it does not define you. You are not what happened to you; what happened to you helped shape you.

Uncovering the wounds of my experience allowed me to own my truth. I was able to break the silence and seek help to heal those wounds. Truth ushers in healing and brings forth freedom. With the years of silence and layers of trauma, there was no way I could go through my healing process alone. There was too much to unpack, but I knew I could no longer be weighed down by the emotional baggage of my past, which was clearly preventing me from becoming a healthier me and sustaining healthy relationships.

I want to remind those of you who may have had an abortion (or abortions) and have been carrying the weight of guilt, grief, shame, and condemnation: You are not alone. You are not the first and you certainly won't be the last. You are forgiven! You are set free! No one can condemn what God has already pardoned! I send you love and hugs through the pages of this book and pray that God touches you right where you are and removes the residue of your past.

Whether you have experienced abortions, sexual, physical, mental, or emotional abuse, or any other traumatic experience, don't allow those experiences to snatch your voice and keep you silent. That's what the enemy wants to do. Be free. Be healed. Be made whole. Keep reading and I'll show you how.

Truth is, trauma may affect you, but it does not define you.

3

BEHIND THE MASK

"Behind every mask there is a face, and behind that a story."

- Marty Rubin

Masks are typically worn to cover up what we're trying to prevent from being exposed. We wear masks to hide our identity and true feelings or pretend to be something we're not. Masks are worn in fear of being found out and showing our true selves (symptoms of Imposter Syndrome). We mask our pain and trauma behind MAC makeup, a smile that brightens up a room, designer bags, nice cars, and big homes that are dark and empty inside because of the lie we're living. I'm not saying that because you have those things that you're masking pain; however, what I am saying is often times, those things can mask feelings of insecurity and grief.

It was August 4, 2007, when I walked down the aisle hand in hand with my mother, as she gave me away in marriage. The church was packed with about 250 guests, the reception turned party was one for the books. After all the months of planning, stressing, and thousands of dollars spent, the day had finally come. What was supposed to be the beginning of an amazing love story and life of togetherness was short-lived and ended three years later in divorce. About nine months into the marriage, we started experiencing challenges that required intervention, so we went to marriage counseling. About three months later, we separated, and the divorce process began.

While I quickly blamed my ex-husband for essentially everything that led up to our divorce, I have since come to understand that I needed to own my part. Whatever I did to him was because of what he did to me. You know that immature tick-for-tack foolishness? Yeah, that! Owning your part doesn't dismiss or excuse the behaviors of others, it's you taking responsibility for your actions. Truth be told, at thirty when we got married, I had not dealt with any of the trauma I had experienced up to that point. I went from one relationship, I mean "situationship," to the next; never addressing any of my previous relational wounds. The unaddressed wound is an unhealed wound. But, in my mind, I was ready. I had a great job, my own home, a nice care, money in the bank—but I was emotionally bankrupt. I had stuff but no capacity to fully avail myself emotionally to him or any man for that matter. Lean in and listen up, marriage doesn't fix what's broken, it exposes it, and that it did! Truth is, I attracted who I was. I had the tendency to connect with men out of my trauma who also had unresolved trauma. This was not healthy and certainly was detrimental to my marriage.

Marriage doesn't fix what's broken, it exposes it.

One of the dimmest and darkest nights of my soul was my season of separation and divorce. I initially did not share what I was going through with anyone. I thought we would work through it in counseling and be fine. As time went on, depression sunk in. Without saying anything to anyone, my immediate family could tell something was wrong. I isolated myself. Didn't want to leave home or be around anyone. I was embarrassed and ashamed that my marriage was failing so early on. Afterall, I didn't get married to get a divorce. Furthermore, I'm Tameka, the minister, woman of faith, seminarian —successful one. Surely, divorce was not on the table. Well, it was.

The emotional toll and weight of this season was unbearable. There were days I could not get out of the bed. I couldn't eat or sleep. I started missing days of work and needed to take time off to try to get myself together. However, getting myself together emotionally was a struggle. One day I decided that I would resign, live off my savings, and eventually start a business or look for work again when things got better. Well, instead of getting better, things got worse. My savings was depleted trying to manage all the bills, including a 745 BMW that was in my name, but my husband drove and stopped paying. I fell behind on the mortgage and other home expenses, credit card payments, and loans. I started receiving foreclosure notices and default payment letters threatening to sue me. My depression grew worse. I became suicidal. The heaviness of all of this in addition to feeling like a complete failure were insurmountable.

I remember thinking, "It's just best that I end it all. I'll just end my life. No one will even notice I'm gone." These thoughts flooded my mind daily. I started to plan out my termination. I never thought to get a gun and shoot myself or hang myself. I considered taking pills but thought what if that didn't work. Then I envisioned how dark Pennsylvania Avenue was at night. Why not drive there —which was not far from my home at all —in the wee hours, pull over on the side, and when a car comes, jump in front of it? They would not even know I was there because I would park on the side of the road with my lights off. The first time I went to do this, I sat in the car patiently around three a.m. I saw a car coming and was ready to follow through with my plan, but, right then, I heard a small still voice whisper, "You will not die; you will live." Wait! What? I closed the car door and wept. Now, you have to understand, God has a sense of humor and what I know is He's really crazy about me (and you, too). How was I able to recognize His voice right in the midst of executing my plan to take my life? Have you ever been in a place in your life where you considered doing something ridiculous and God blocked it? Listen!!! Who wouldn't serve a God like this! Praise break! God will block what was meant to take you out.

Well, you would think that I would have dismissed the suicidal thoughts and attempts, rebuke the devil, declare and decree, pray and fast, and fight for my life after hearing God's voice. Oh, but, NO! My situation didn't change; in fact, the letters continued to come, a foreclosure notice stuck to my screen door. On top of that, I was plagued with thoughts of how my marriage spiraled so quicky, and how I was losing everything I had worked so hard to get. Nothing I owned was in my ex-husband's name. I had worked hard and saved during my early to mid-twenties. Can you imagine how devastated I was? Not to mention how angry I was at God? I was furious! The suicidal thoughts crept back in. I felt like I was having a Job moment where he lost everything he had. This faithful, upright man of God lost it all. His children, livestock, investments; he lost it all. But the thing is, God gave the devil permission and said, "Have you considered my servant Job?" (Job 1:8 NIV) The encouragement and hope is in how Job handled the situation and how God turned it all around in Job 42 (NIV). I'll talk more about how God turned my situation around later in the book.

I set out two more times to end it all. Low and behold, that same small, still voice spoke each time and said, "You will not die; you will live." I thought, *What if God allows me to live and I end up paralyzed and have to explain to people that I got like that because I attempted to kill myself?* I couldn't stomach that thought especially knowing God already said I would not die. So, the third time was the final time that I drove myself back home and began to deal with what was before me. For those of you who may have struggled with suicidal ideation, are wrestling with the thoughts, or have survived an attempt, God is not through with you yet. He loves you. You shall LIVE and not die!

According to the CDC, suicide is the 10th leading cause of death in the US. In 2019, 47,511 Americans died by suicide.[iii] These statistics are grueling to say the least. No one is exempt from the pressures of life. You may be facing your own personal Tsunami but look up to the hills from whence cometh your help. God is with you and there are resources and professional help available to aide you (see the Resources page). You were not built to break. You were built to stand.

My choice to live didn't stop the heartache and struggles. As a result of my divorce, my home foreclosed, I filed bankruptcy, and one of my cars was repossessed —the one my ex-husband drove, since he stopped paying the note, I did too. God graced me to still have my car to drive because I paid it off two years after purchasing it new. For my peace and sanity, I was willing to let it all go and trust that God would give me a Job 42 testimony of restoration. I was no longer willing to pretend I was okay while dying inside. I was not willing to hold on to anything that was already over. I eventually told my family what was going on, everyone met at my house to help me pack and load things to storage. I went forth with the bankruptcy proceedings, finalized the divorce, and prepared to live life in its new normal.

I now needed to find a new place to live and a new job. After battling depression, finding it difficult to get out of the bed to go anywhere, I resigned from my job. I was in transition. I was homeless. While I didn't go to a shelter, it certainly crossed my mind. Family and friends opened their door. Initially, I stayed with my cousins for about a month, sleeping on the top bunk of one of their daughter's beds. Afterward, I stayed with another cousin for several months before getting a note on the bed saying I had to move in thirty days. The note didn't give much detail, but she later explained she was relocating. I left there and found myself renting a room from a friend for almost a year. At that time, I secured a new job making just enough to pay my room rent, car insurance, gas, and a few groceries. Oh, but I remember the days during my transition when I wasn't working and had no income. My family would slide a few dollars in my hand for gas and call me over for dinner a few times. I pawned my wedding ring just for a few dollars. It was the absolute lowest season of my entire life. But you couldn't tell.

I remember praying and seeking God for one thing: stability. I was appreciative of the new job and my friend's generosity in letting me rent a room, but I wanted my home. I was ready to start over and rebuild. What was behind me was behind me. I was ready for what was ahead. It's the resiliency in all of us that causes us to work harder and push upward as we bounce back. It wasn't long after praying for stability and specifically asking for my own place that God opened a door for me to get an apartment. I was specific about where I wanted to live and what type of community I wanted to live in. And He granted me my request. Won't he do it? Yes, He will! It was a new community, covered garage parking, with exceptional amenities, where I felt safe and could enjoy my peace. With all the chaos I experienced, I needed some peace.

The saying "you don't look like what you've been through," that was definitely me. I was still driving nice and dressing well. I kept driving that paid-for white Mercedes. I wore my mink and furs in the winter, dressed to the nines and not missing a beat, with designer bags on my shoulder, and a fake smile on my face. The smile, the car, and the clothes were all just a mask. Behind the mask was a broken, wounded warrior who was determined to fight for her life and give the devil a black eye while doing so. Behind the mask was a deeply depressed and distressed woman with faith that this wasn't the end, but that God would turn it around to work in her favor. Masking the shame, embarrassment, and fear of the unknown became too much. I had to remove the mask in order to face my truth. I encourage you to do the same.

What I've learned is that masks aren't worn just on Halloween or during a global pandemic. Masks are worn by the most successful, impactful leaders and influencers every day. Masks are worn by family and friends that we think we know well. Masks are worn by me and you. Masks have become many people's norms. When we mask the truth of our lives and experiences with lies, self-sabotaging behaviors, and the fear of being found out, we keep ourselves in bondage. We are captive to the lie which prevents us from living in truth.

REFLECTION

Now that I've shared my experiences with you, I want you to pause and reflect over your life and your experiences. Take a few moments before moving on to the next section to write down any thoughts, emotions, takeaways, or triggers you may have experienced. Consider how you may wear masks to hide your own trauma or situation. Think about how you overcame a personal tragedy or depression.

_____

_____

_____

_____

_____

_____

_____

_____

_____

_____

_____

_____

_____

_____

_____

_____

_____

_____

Have you ever masked your pain, trauma, or emotions? How do you wear masks to stay hidden?

_____

_____

_____

_____

_____

_____

_____

_____

_____

_____

_____

_____

_____

_____

_____

_____

_____

_____

_____

_____

_____

_____

_____

_____

_____

_____

PART II

———

ROADMAP TO HEALING
AND RECOVERY

"Healing is your right, your responsibility, and the risk you can't
afford not to take." -Thaiia Senquetta

4
—————

LET THE HEALING BEGIN

"He heals the brokenhearted and binds up their wounds."

- Psalm 147:3, NIV

S o, *how do I heal, Tameka?* That answer may look different to you. Healing is a very personal process. There is no one-size-fits all approach, but there are general methods you can start with. When we have experienced trauma, it is imperative that we seek mental health and emotional wellness support to help us navigate through our healing process to become well again. Often times, especially in the African American community, we neglect our mental and emotional health. We have experienced racial and community trauma as well as personal trauma but refuse to get the appropriate support to help us heal these insurmountable wounds.

There are a few fundamentals I want you to keep in mind when it comes to healing. It is a process. It is a journey. It is uncomfortable, but it is necessary. I have to tell you on the onset, get comfortable with being uncomfortable. Sometimes the healing hurts more than the wound. You have to be willing to put in the work if you want it to work. Be patient with yourself and give yourself grace. Don't try to heal on your own. You'll discover that there are layers to healing. When you begin to pull back one layer, there are several more that you have to go through to get to the root. I urge you to seek support from a coach, counselor, clergy, or clinician to walk with you on this journey. Get support from those who are professionally trained to provide tools and strategies that you can apply to your life.

Sometimes the healing hurts more than the wound.

Because I advocate for faith and mental health, I knew my healing journey could not be void of my faith and my relationship with God. I sought Him in prayer and flipped through the pages of the Bible to pull healing Scriptures that I meditated on and recited daily. I invited and welcomed Him into my process. While my therapist provided weekly tools and strategies, God guided me daily.

In this section, I share the roadmap to healing and recovery which is a self-help guide developed out of my personal healing journey and professional experiences working with clients. This roadmap serves as a guide for you to follow as you begin your healing journey. This is only a guide. I urge you to seek additional support to help with your specific healing goals and needs.

Before we get to the roadmap in chapters 5-7, here is a framework and tools I find helpful when beginning your healing journey.

A.I.M. Method (Admit. Invite. Make.)

ADMIT THAT YOU ARE HURTING. **Invite God and invoke the Holy Spirit. Make healing a priority.**

The A.I.M. Method provides three basic steps to beginning your healing journey. These are steps I took when I decided it was time to heal and deal. As simple as they may seem, they are crucial to the foundation that establishes the trajectory of your journey. As you aim for healing and wholeness, keep these steps in mind and let them set the course to reach your goal.

Step 1

The first step to healing is to *admit that you are hurting*. No more pretending to be okay, hiding behind the wound and suppressing your feelings. Don't deny the pain the injury has caused you. Truth is, most times it oozes out of your pours without you even realizing it. It's in the way you respond and react to various situations. Like when you go from zero to a thousand in 1.5 seconds and the person on the receiving end is trying to figure out what's wrong with you? Listen, I've been there, and I know I'm not alone. This happens when we perceive a threat and feel unsafe. We become emotionally roused and unable to regulate those emotions quickly. We find ourselves in fight, flight, or freeze mode in order to find safety by protecting ourselves. This is called trauma response.

Another way the pain oozes out of your pores is through your connections. Who you choose to connect with may be a direct result of unresolved trauma and wounds. You may find yourself in unhealthy attachments with your abuser or perpetrator thinking that one day their behavior will change. This is trauma bonding. According to Medical News Today, "A trauma bond is a connection between an abusive person and the individual being abused. It typically occurs when the abused person begins to develop sympathy or affection for the abuser."[iv] This may show up in relationships with family, friends, or partners. Many times, instead of admitting that we are hurting, we react and respond out of the pain we've experienced as well as attach ourselves to people who are abusive (physically, verbally, mentally, emotionally, or sexually).

Step 2

The second step is to *invite God and invoke the Holy Spirit* into your healing process. As I mentioned before, you can't do this healing work on your own. Inviting God on your healing journey is critical to experiencing great victory over your trauma. Recognizing and acknowledging that you need Him every step of the way releases the control you may think you have on this journey. Invoking the Holy Spirit gives Him free reign to uproot, reveal, and comfort you along the way. In Luke 5:31, we are reminded that "those who are well have no need of a physician, but those who are sick [do]." (Luke 5:31 ESV) We are in need of the Great Physician, the ultimate Healer, Jehovah Rapha. Once you have admitted that you are hurting, invite God and Holy Spirit in and let them lead the way.

One way that you can invite God and invoke the Holy Spirit on your journey is through prayer. Prayer is that two-way communication with God. It is not a monologue but a dialogue. After I prayed, I listened to hear what God had to say. Through prayer, He began to show me those areas that were tender and needed specialized attention. He kissed my wounds with his healing salve and reminded me He was right there with me. He reminded me through Psalm 147:3 that "He heals the brokenhearted and binds up their wounds." (Psalm 147:3 NIV) I was reminded that healing is an option that's available to me and is my birthright. I was reminded through prayer of all of the instances in the Bible where He healed and that I, too, can be healed. He whispered, "Daughter, do you want to be healed?" And I replied, "Yes, my Lord."

Prayer connects us with God. Invite God the Father, Son, and Holy Spirit on your journey to not only guide you but to uproot every seed of trauma that has been planted. After the uprooting comes the rebuilding. We are reminded in Jeremiah 30:17, "But I will restore you to health and heal your wounds, declares the Lord."(Jeremiah 30:17 NIV) As you pray, be open to the voice of God and the ways He speaks to you. He's there to help guide you.

My healing journey initially began around December 2019 with prayer and supplication to God. I was very aware of my story and personal experiences. I knew the pain I endured and the numbness I felt as a result of it. I knew the dark secrets I held close and were taking to my grave. I realized just how much all of this was impacting me emotionally. I recognized how the impact of my personal trauma and unhealed wounds played out in repeated unhealthy relationships and bad choices and decisions. I could never understand how I mastered success in every area of my life except relationships. Finally, I began to pray and seek God for real. I prayed a three-word prayer that simply said, **"Show me, me."** I wanted God to reveal the deep parts that were untouched. I really wanted Him to heal all the hurt and pain from my past. I sought His forgiveness concerning all past and present marks I missed. I needed to get to the root of my dysfunction, and prayer paved the way.

Step 3

The third step is to *make healing a priority*. Whatever we deem a priority we give our attention to. This is what we focus on. If you are serious about healing those unspoken wounds, you must make healing a priority. This requires three things: commitment, consistency, and intentionality. Commitment is a non-negotiable. You have to be committed to the process and doing the work in order to get the results you desire. It is not your coach, counselor, clergy, or clinician's job to do the work for you. Their job is to provide you with the tools; your job is to use them. Consistency on this journey is key. You have to show up for your healing even when you don't feel like it. Consistency yields results. Setting your intentions daily around the healing work that you have set out to do helps you to stay focused and keep the main thing the main thing. When healing is a priority, you will do whatever it takes to reach this goal. This includes seeking professional support.

As I continued to pray and the Lord continued to reveal areas of brokenness, He guided me to therapy. Now, I had been to therapy years prior. But it wasn't until I got serious about my healing and I was committed to the process that therapy began to work for me. I had to put in the hard work to get the results I desired —healing AND wholeness! Like Dr. Anita Phillips says, "Prayer is a weapon and therapy is a strategy."

*"Prayer is a weapon and therapy
is a strategy."*

Therapy helps bring awareness, provides tools, and creates a safe space that is nonjudgmental. My therapist helped me to acknowledge, identify, and name my experiences. I recall opening up to her to share some of my experiences. She was the first person to help me identify my experiences as "traumatic." If you could have seen my face when she said, "That was pretty traumatic." My heart dropped. I had always associated that term with the military or a really bad accident where individuals had to be medevacked to a hospital. No wonder I did not make the connection previously. I chopped up my experience as just life and something I went through. I did not want to accept the fact that I had experienced anything associated with trauma. I was in denial and had pretended to be okay for so long, when in fact, I was broken, emotionally detached and underdeveloped. Broken people break people, and that's exactly what my cycles and patterns of behaviors displayed.

Broken people break people.

Building Your Toolkit

While you are on your healing journey, it's essential to build your tool kit which helps you with processing emotions, grounding, and self-regulating when you become emotionally stimulated. Here are a few healing tools that have been tested and proven to get you the results you desire and bring you to a place of healing: journaling, affirmations, and mindfulness.

Journaling

Journaling is one of the most therapeutic tools you can use. It allows you to process your feelings and emotions by writing them out. Don't bottle them up; let them out on the page. This helps you to release suppressed feelings and emotions. Journaling your thoughts help you manage your emotions, reduce stress, and cope with anxiety and depression. Journaling serves as a tracking system that helps chronical your thoughts, fears, concerns as well as recognize some of your triggers, negative thoughts, and behaviors. I also recommend journaling your successes while healing. This allows you a moment to pause, recognize your growth, and celebrate the progress you have made.

While journaling is a normal practice for me, it became an essential part of my healing journey. I began to put my thoughts, emotions, progress, and experiences on paper, journaling almost daily. From this practice, I began to outline my journey and started to write this book. The practice of journaling brings healing. It also provides opportunities for your creativity to flow and open doors for you to express your thoughts and perhaps share your story with the world.

Affirmations

Another powerful healing tool I use and often share with clients are words of affirmation. Affirmations are positive statements you write and speak over yourself. These statements help you overcome those negative thoughts you may have about yourself as a result of your experiences. They also combat self-sabotaging thoughts and behaviors. The goal is to repeat them until you believe them. Sometimes you will have to dig deeper into the affirmations you are speaking over yourself and ask questions in order for you to authentically believe what you are speaking over your life. If you say, "I am enough," then ask yourself "why am I enough or what makes me enough?" Once you begin to believe what you are saying about yourself, you replace those negative thoughts with positive ones and begin to see positive change manifest. You will soon see your self-esteem boosted and positive self-talk becoming your norm. Here are examples of a few affirmations:

- I give myself permission to heal, to feel, and to deal with the parts of me that hurt the most.

- I release myself from anything or anyone that no longer serves me well.
- My value is not determined by what others think of me.
- I forgive myself for what I didn't know.

Mindfulness Meditation

Several years ago, I was introduced to mindfulness meditation and have implemented this into daily practice as a way of centering myself. Mindfulness meditation trains us to become more mindful throughout the day, particularly during difficult situations. I recommend this practice as a healing tool because it requires you to focus on your breathing and be present in the moment. This is a great way to ground yourself whenever you are triggered, feeling stressed or anxious, or simply need to relax. While practicing mindfulness, you may feel yourself drifting and wandering in your thoughts. This is normal. Simply bring your thoughts back to the present moment and breathe. Mindfulness meditation allows you to quiet your thoughts, shift your attention to the present, and free yourself of any judgment.

The healing tools and strategies presented in this chapter are provided to better equip you as you embark upon or continue your healing journey. As you dig deeper into the trauma of your past, apply these principles and receive the healing your heart desires and your life deserves.

5

FACE YOUR TRUTH

"To thine own self be true." -William Shakespeare

When you look in the mirror, what do you see? I'll wait. Actually, I want you to grab a mirror or head over to one and look at yourself. What do you see when you see yourself? Write down your responses. Most times we list all the positive qualities and admire our own beauty. For some, this is a difficult exercise to do because it requires you to face some hard truths about who you were pretending to be, and who you really are. Some see hurt and pain in their eyes. Some see scars that serve as a reminder of the abuse. Some see the little girl or little boy who was neglected, abandoned, and rejected. Some see what you refused to see.

The first stop on the roadmap to recovery is a hard stop. Slow down, pull over, and place your car in park. Here is where you have to *face your truth*. In order to face your truth, you have to face yourself. This is where you actually remove the mask or lift the veil. In order to heal, you have to face the truth of your experiences, the pain of your past, and the wounds that remain unspoken. Lean in and listen up. You can't fix what you don't face. Facing the truth of your trauma requires you to acknowledge who injured you, identify the source of your pain, and name your trauma. What's *your* trauma? What's *your* truth? Facing your truth uncovers the lies you have lived with for so long. It exposes the realities of a story you fabricated. It uproots the secrets you hid and were determined to take to your grave. Facing your truth also releases you from the bondage of your past and lightens the burden so you can be free.

You can't fix what you don't face.

Acknowledging who injured you and identifying the source of your trauma is necessary in facing the truth of it. Oftentimes, we don't want to face the reality of what others have done to us. We prefer not to mention their names and depending on the severity of the trauma, not even see their faces. The "who and what" are important aspects of facing the truth so that you no longer live the lie or hide in shame. The truth exposes the lie you have been telling yourself, uproots shame and guilt, and allows you to heal and grow. It is time to take back the power the perpetrator, abuser, or offender took from you.

When you face your truth, you also have to *name your trauma*. For so long, I referred to rape as "unconsented sex." The abortion was simply "the biggest sin and disappointment to God." The divorce was "we're no longer together." A huge part of the healing process is being able to name it. I'm not sure what your traumatic experience was but begin to name it. Take your power back and snatch your voice back. Rape. Abortion. Divorce. Attempted suicide. Abuse. Neglect. Abandonment. Poverty. Prostitution. And the list goes on. No longer will you minimize your truth and the effect it has on you. You will face it by naming it.

For twenty-five years, I referred to my experience as unconsented sex. While that is what it was, it has a name. Instead of naming it, I defined it. That made it feel less harsh. I didn't want to accept the fact that I was a victim of rape. I minimized it because I knew my predator and didn't want to view him as such. I had heard of many other stories of rape, but it didn't fit my personal experience; therefore, in my mind, it was something that happened and I just wanted it to go away so I can move on with my life, finish college, and pursue my career.

During one of my sessions, my therapist gave me an assignment to create a timeline of my relationships from the first relationship to the present. When we reconvened the following week, we started discussing my timeline and got stuck on the first relationship. I began to share that experience in detail for the very first time in my life. This is where I discovered it was my experiences with that relationship that began a pattern of unhealthy relationships. One of the assessments my therapist made was, "Tameka, you were not emotionally ready to handle relationships due to unresolved trauma," I thought, "Go figure!" This all began to make sense to me. My awareness was heightened. Now, I have to tell you how uncomfortable this was for me. As we continued through the timeline over the next several sessions, I had to pace myself. I felt triggered by the memories and even had flashbacks, but I also felt safe because I had someone to help process those emotions.

I realized I was doing what many of us do when it comes to relationships and have unresolved trauma. We rebound. We call ourselves "moving on" when really, we haven't gone anywhere except to a new man or woman with a different name but same issues. We transfer our issues on to the next person and create unhealthy attachments out of our trauma, as well as theirs. We attract who we are, not who we pretend to be. We can no longer pretend to be who we are not. We have to release the fear of being found out and face the truth about who we are, what we've gone through, and how it made us feel.

Another revelation I received in facing the truth of my abortion is that there was an abortive spirit lurking over me. I couldn't figure out for the life of me why I would start things and find it extremely difficult to see it to fruition. I would get to a certain point of working my vision, producing great content, putting things in motion for implementation and execution, then stop. End it. Abort the assignment. It almost happened with this book. I literally stopped writing for months and moved on to something else. The Holy Spirit arrested my attention and made it clear as day that what I have been contending with for years is an abortive spirit. At this point, I picked up my computer and proceeded to finish this book. I made a decision from that moment forward that I will finish what I start.

When facing the dark, ugly truth of your experiences, you begin to shed light and expose what was hidden. You are able to dispel the lies you've told yourself over and over again. This, my friends, is where recovery begins.

On the next page, take some time to reflect over what you've read. Breathe. Don't rush through it. Write your thoughts as you begin to face your truth. Use this space to acknowledge who or what hurt you, name your trauma, and identify how it made you feel.

REFLECTION

When you look in the mirror, what do you see? How does this make you feel?

_____

_____

_____

_____

_____

_____

_____

_____

_____

_____

_____

_____

_____

_____

_____

_____

_____

_____

Name your trauma here. What is the "thing" you are recovering from?

_____

_____

_____

_____

_____

_____

_____

_____

_____

_____

_____

_____

_____

_____

_____

_____

_____

_____

_____

_____

_____

_____

6

FEEL WHAT YOU FEEL

"Feel what you need to feel and then let it go.

Do not let it consume you." -Dhiman

Brace yourself for this next stop. In fact, I need you to keep driving at a nice steady pace, blast your favorite song, and bop your head to the beat before you pull over for this next stop. I have "Just Fine" by Mary J. Blige playing to get me right for this next stop. Ok, here we go. Take the exit, pull over slowly, put your car in park, and exhale. The next stop on the roadmap to recovery is the ability to *feel what you feel*. Yep, let's talk about these feelings! You're probably starting to cringe right now. Many of us have a hard time expressing how we feel, especially when it comes to trauma. We have suppressed those feelings for so long and pushed them so far down that we rather not deal with them at all. Ohhh, but if we're going to heal for real, we have to get into these feelings. Feelings are not facts; they are the emotional responses to something that has happened. While they are not facts, they should be validated.

If you're like me, you were taught to be strong. Tough it out. Never let 'em see you sweat. I was good at telling you off but sucked at really telling you how I felt emotionally. For most of my life, I felt emotionally unsafe, especially in relationships, due to my traumatic experiences. I felt like I needed to protect myself and guard my heart from being hurt and wounded, all to end up even more hurt and wounded. I built walls and tried to control situations and people. This all prevented me from fully expressing my true feelings. Can you relate? I challenge you, as my therapist did me, to think about how you define strength. Who and what experiences taught you how to be strong or what strength is? If you had to define strength now, what would it be? For me, strength is weakness redefined. It is being able to fully express your true feelings and emotions. It is vulnerability at its best.

Feeling what you feel requires a level of vulnerability many of us would rather bypass: Opening up to admit that what they did hurt you; what happened to you scorned you; that the situation angered you, upset you, disappointed you. Having to sit with and in the shame and guilt...no, we'd rather camouflage our true feelings than dig them up and sit in them so we can heal.

Suppressing those feelings do more damage than good. Instead of suppressing your emotions, address them, process them, and release them.

When addressing your emotions, you shift from a head space to a heart space. The matters of the heart are free to speak without withholding how you really feel. When you begin to sit in these emotions, you can now begin to process them. You may need to talk it out or even write it out. If you feel tears welling up, don't fight back, release them. These tears are cleansing that space and making room for your true emotions to emerge. Don't be afraid to feel. Feel what you feel.

For me, this was the most challenging on the recovery road. I remember when I would talk about my trauma and feel myself becoming emotional, how I would pretend to be unbothered, feeling like I was about to explode. I can hear my therapist saying now, "Breathe." And every time I heard her say it, I would exhale and give that breath sound and most times tears followed. I had built so many walls and there were so many layers to break through. I gave my therapist a run for her money, but I'm so glad she was there to help chip away at the walls until they came down and peeled back the layers, one layer at a time. I eventually felt safe enough to sit in my feelings and process them in a healthy way.

Feeling what you feel requires you to do three things: name your feelings, process your emotions, and release them. When naming your feelings, think about how the experience made you feel as well as how you feel when you think about the experience.

Oftentimes, feelings of guilt, shame, bitterness, anger, sadness, and fear are associated with traumatic experiences. These feelings may worsen when untreated and lead to anxiety and depression. Here is where I highly recommend seeking a clinician to help provide therapeutic services to help you navigate these emotions. It can be quite uncomfortable to process your emotions. Sitting in and with your emotions may cause you to retreat and stop the healing process. I encourage you to press through this step. Being honest about how you feel requires a level of vulnerability that ultimately brings peace. This peace you experience helps you to release those emotions and move forward without holding on to negative emotions. When you are able to name your feelings, process your emotions, and release them, you will find yourself well on your way on the path to healing and wholeness.

On this stop, it is also important to identify your triggers. It's difficult to process what you don't first identify. Triggers, or reminders of a past trauma, show up in many ways and affect us all differently. One of my triggers is hearing of someone who died by suicide. I'm reminded of the times I attempted to take my own life. At times, I find myself becoming overwhelmed by sadness and even grief. What are some of your triggers as it relates to your experiences? When you are aware of your triggers and able to identify them, you are in a position to self-regulate. The key here is being able to ground yourself so that you can regulate the emotions that were roused due to the trigger. Some ways you can ground yourself are taking a walk, breathing techniques, connecting with the earth, praying, and meditating, to name a few.

I mentioned earlier that baby dedications were a trigger for me. For about a year or so, my emotions would be all over the place thinking about the child I chose not to keep. I would feel those emotions welling up inside, totally taking control of my entire body. I would have to sit through this ceremony praying that it would be over soon. I recall the pastor giving the parents, grandparents, and godparents their charge; handing them roses and explaining what they represented; then ending with a prayer. At the end of the prayer and benediction, I would let out a sigh of relief but was never totally relieved. I would go home and just cry. At that time, I didn't know how to effectively process my emotions. Eventually, they went away. I buried them. There may come a time when those buried emotions come back to haunt you, but not in a bad, spooky way. They are resurrected in order for you to heal and deal so that you don't have to take them to your grave. Instead, be brave enough to confront them, confuse the enemy, and take control over that part of your life.

As you work through the steps on this stop, lean into that vulnerable space and allow the Holy Spirit to rest right there with you. There is safety in the arms of the One who already knows your true feelings. You may need to write a letter or note to yourself or the person who hurt you in order get those emotions out; then throw it away. Don't suppress the feelings, release them. Cry if you have to. The goal is to get you to tap into those emotions and release them.

REFLECTION

Now that you have named your trauma, how did this trauma make you feel?

_____

_____

_____

_____

_____

_____

_____

_____

_____

_____

_____

_____

_____

_____

_____

_____

_____

_____

_____

_____

In what ways will you overcome these feelings? *Use tips you've learned from the book.

_____

_____

_____

_____

_____

_____

_____

_____

_____

_____

_____

_____

_____

_____

_____

_____

_____

_____

_____

_____

_____

_____

7

FORGIVE AND FORGET

"Forgetting those things which are behind and reaching forward
to those things which are ahead." -Philippians 3:13, NKJV

O kay, do me a favor and breathe! The title of this chapter
may cause some to have heart palpitations, but I need
you to relax and read this chapter slowly and process
it deeply. Forgiveness takes prayer, grace, and a mindset shift.
Transparently, forgiving my ex-husband was extremely difficult
for me to do. There were times when I wanted to take matters into
my own hands. I wanted my perpetrators to suffer for the damage,
losses, and pain they caused me. I wanted revenge. It was Romans
12:19 that reminded me, "Dear friends, never take revenge. Leave

that to the righteous anger of God. For the Scriptures say, "I will take revenge; I will pay them back, says the Lord." (Romans 12:19 NLT)

When we have been mishandled, hurt, or wounded, the thought of forgiving is farthest from our mind. While it may be difficult to conceptualize the thought, there is power in forgiving. This isn't an easy step; however, it is necessary for your healing, freedom, and growth. The power lies within you, and now it is time to pull it out of you. I do not recommend you attempting to work through this area of healing until you have worked through the previous steps. This is the last stop on the journey but requires patience, perseverance, and intentionality.

I think it's important to establish a fundamental understanding about forgiveness. This understanding transforms the way we think about forgiveness which in turn helps us apply this concept to our healing journey. To forgive is to release an offender of any wrongdoing. Forgiveness is a choice. It's you choosing to no longer hold on to the negative emotions associated with the behavior or act your offender caused. It's choosing to release them so that you can be free from the bondage of your emotions. Now, is this easy to do? Absolutely not. However, when you make the choice to forgive, you chart your path to healing and recovery from the wounded version of you. Forgiveness is not about the other person; it's for you. Forgiveness does not excuse the behavior or condone the actions of the person who offended you. It does, however, extend the grace you need to release yourself and the person who harmed you. When you don't forgive, you allow that person to maintain control. I don't know about you, but the way my control issues are set up —well, I'm actually working on this now that I have an awareness of where my control issues come from —I don't want anything or anyone controlling me, so I decided I would go ahead and forgive those who harmed or offended me. Forgiveness relinquishes the control the person had on you and your emotions.

Forgiveness is not predicated on an apology being extended, but on your willingness to pardon even without an apology. Sometimes an apology is not rendered. If you are waiting on an apology in order to forgive, you may be waiting forever. The person who owes you an apology may be deceased or one you may never see or hear from again. Will you then hold on to unforgiveness and carry the resentment and anger for the rest of your life, or will you choose to forgive, let it go, and be free? The choice is yours. When you choose to forgive, you in turn are forgiven by our Heavenly Father. Scripture reminds us, "And when you stand praying, if you hold anything against anyone, forgive them, so that your Father in heaven may forgive you your sins" (Mark 11:25 NIV). Here we are challenged to forgive so that we, too, can be forgiven. And I don't know about you, but I need the Father's forgiveness.

Another thought to consider about forgiveness is that it does not require reconciliation. You are not obligated to reconcile with an abuser, perpetrator, or offender. If you chose to reconcile, be sure to establish healthy boundaries and realistic expectations of how you are to be treated going forward. Boundaries are established to protect and maintain a healthy mental and emotional state. As an important side note, if abuse is present, I highly recommend you seek professional support or contact local authorities.

Not only is it important to forgive others, but it's imperative that you forgive yourself. Oftentimes we hold on to the guilt and shame of our experiences and hold ourselves hostage. Many find it difficult to forgive themselves for the choices they have made and what happened to them. Forgiving yourself brings freedom. Forgive yourself for what you didn't know; for what wasn't your fault; for what you had no control over. Understand that the moment you ask the Father for forgiveness, you are forgiven. When I grasped this understanding, a weight was lifted off my shoulder. It's freeing to forgive others, but even more freeing to forgive yourself.

Forgiveness is a process and takes time. Don't rush through this step but keep the fundamentals of forgiveness in mind. As I gained a clearer understanding of forgiveness and shifted my mindset, it became easier for me to forgive my father for his absence. I was able to get to this place prior to speaking with him back in 2019, when he apologized for his physical and emotional absence and told me how proud he was of me. The person who sexually abused me and my ex-husband never apologized; however, I have forgiven them both because I understand this is what I needed to do to obtain the healing I desired. My challenge to you is that while you are on your healing journey, you would consider the power of forgiveness and choose to forgive so that you can be free. Peter asked, "Lord, how many times shall I forgive my brother and sister who sins against me? Up to seven times?" And the Lord replied, "I tell you, not seven times, but seventy times seven" (Matthew 18: 21-22 NIV). When you choose to forgive, you will find yourself one step closer on your healing journey.

Forgetting What Lies Behind

"Forget what happened in the past, and do not dwell on events from long ago." Isaiah 43:18, GW

This scripture certainly stretches many of us to a greater level of discomfort. As if processing forgiveness wasn't enough, right? By no means do I suggest that forgetting is easy to do. In fact, naturally, we are inclined to recall things because we all have a memory. However, on this journey to healing, with the end goal being peace, freedom, and optimal emotional wellness, we must shift our focus to the ultimate prize —victory over the enemy of our past.

Forgetting doesn't mean you don't have a memory but that you choose not to dwell on what held you captive and kept you bound. When you choose to forget, you no longer focus on what happened, but your primary focus becomes how to heal from it.

The longer you dwell on what happened, the longer it takes for you to move forward in a healthy way. The unhealed and unprocessed thoughts and emotions attached to the memories prevent us from receiving the peace we long for. I must caution you, though. Forgetting can be dangerous if you have not carefully navigated through the healing process with a mental health professional who can guide you along. Without this level of support, you run the risk of not fully dealing with the truth of the experience or emotions associated with what you experienced; potentially neglecting the parts of you that truly need to heal and avoiding doing the work necessary to heal. You may in turn do more damage than good.

For me, choosing to forgive and forget were liberating. I gained such a peace. You know, the kind that surpasses all of your understanding. Not dwelling on the experiences of my past opened my heart to receive the new things God wanted to do in my life; the new story He was preparing me to share that would help others like you. Of course, I remember being abandoned, sexually abused, terminating my pregnancy, and ending my marriage, but when I made healing my priority, worked through the process with a professional, and prayed for my perpetrators, then I was able to forgive, forget, and forge ahead releasing the shackles that held me bound.

REFLECTION

List the name(s) of those you need to forgive.

_____

_____

_____

_____

_____

_____

_____

_____

_____

_____

_____

_____

_____

_____

_____

_____

_____

_____

_____

_____

_____

_____

Based on what you have learned about forgiving and forgetting in this chapter, what are three nuggets that will help you forgive those you listed?

_____

_____

_____

_____

_____

_____

_____

_____

_____

_____

_____

_____

_____

_____

_____

_____

_____

_____

_____

_____

_____

_____

_____

How does forgiving and forgetting benefit you? If this is a
challenging step for you, be sure to note that, too.

_____

_____

_____

_____

_____

_____

_____

_____

_____

_____

_____

_____

_____

_____

_____

_____

_____

_____

_____

_____

_____

_____

_____

_____

_____

_____

PART III

GREAT VICTORY!

"It doesn't matter who you are, where you come from. The ability to triumph begins with you – always." -Oprah Winfrey

8

BE FREE AND MOVE FORWARD

"So, if the Son sets you free, you will be free indeed." John 8:36, NIV

"The righteous keep moving forward..." Job 17:9, NLT

On the other side of trauma is triumph. In order to experience great victory over trauma, you have to go through the process of healing. Just because you have overcome or survived a situation does not mean you are healed from it. When you are healed, there is a freedom that follows and allows you to move forward in a healthy way.

My healing journey exposed some of the dark, ugly truths about areas of my life I kept silent about. More than anything, I wanted to break free and release the pain of my past. While on my healing journey, as I became more aware of my trauma and its effects, and learned strategies and skills to help me heal, my shell began to crack, walls began to come down, and I begin to see the breaking of day. Eventually I found myself on the other side of bondage, experiencing a freedom I had never known. I started moving to a new beat with every step I took toward a brighter day.

Freedom is one of the benefits of healing. You are no longer bound to the pain of your past or the wounds from the experience. This kind of freedom brings relief from the stronghold of your emotions. You are free from the secrets, self-sabotaging behaviors, and survival mode techniques. Freedom allows you to be your authentic self. You experience a peace that surpasses all of your understanding, joy everlasting, and a love that flows in you and out to others.

This newfound freedom helps me to make better choices and respond differently than when I was broken and wounded. When you are free, you are no longer controlled by your feelings, and you learn to manage your emotions. There is great victory found in freedom. You realize you have defeated not just the enemy of your experience, but of your emotions. Freedom holds great value. When you add up the cost of all you went through and the price you paid, you'll begin to walk in your freedom unapologetically.

There are those who are used to seeing you broken and bound that they won't know how to handle you healed and free. That's totally fine. Healing becomes offensive to those who benefited from your brokenness. Freedom opens up opportunities to make new associations and healthy connections. This freedom leaves no residue of your past. The chains have been loosed. You can smile again, dance in the rain, and enjoy life free of false pretenses. Here is where your soul finds freedom. Your mind, emotions, and spirit are healed and align perfectly.

When you're free you're able to bask in unspeakable joy, uninterrupted peace, and an undeniable love for yourself. These are the byproducts of freedom. We aim to live a life of joy and peace. How do you get to this place of freedom after experiencing trauma? By making healing a priority and committing to the process. Understanding that "whom the Son sets free, is free indeed."(John 8:36 NIV) When God sets you free, there is no one or nothing that can keep you bound.

In the words of one of the greatest civil rights leaders of all times, Rev. Dr. Martin Luther King, Jr., that ring loudly as I pen the words to this chapter, "Free at last, free at last, thank God almighty, we are free at last." You, too, will be able to utter these same words once you have done the healing work necessary to usher you over to the other side of trauma.

Moving Forward

I read a particular passage in the Bible in Job, which reminded me that "the righteous keep moving forward."(Job 17:9 NLT) Notice it did not say keep moving on. When you move on, there is residue of your past because you haven't done the healing work. When you move forward, there is no resemblance of what you came out of. Sometimes, while on the journey to healing, you may be tempted to go back to that place of familiarity; that comfortable state of complacency. But I admonish you to keep moving forward! The only time you look back is to see how far God has brought you. Your best life begins with a single step in the right direction— forward. Forward is where you create a new narrative, gain a new perspective, and discover a new identity.

When you create a new narrative, you no longer write your story as a victim but as a victor. You are no longer afraid to tell your story. You are free enough to share your experience and tell others how they, too, can overcome. That great victory you now know is what you want others to experience. Healing brings forth a new perspective on life. When you were wounded, broken, and bound, you thought that is how you had to live. You bought in to the lies that this was how you would always be. On the other side of healing, your point of view has changed. You know that healing is available to you. That it is God's desire for you to be healed. That there is life after trauma and it's worth living. When you move forward after healing the hurt and pain of your past, you discover a new you. You no longer have to live behind the mask, the disguise, and the lies. Your identity is found in Christ. You are not what happened to you; you are who God says you are. You are fearfully and wonderfully made. You are more than a conqueror.

Once you have overcome trauma and have healed from its effects, there is a freedom that awaits you and allows you to move forward in a new way. I started out sharing my story of trauma and talking about the unspoken wounds that silenced me for years. I transitioned you to the roadmap the helps bring healing and transformation. Now we are here on the other side of trauma — the place of great victory!

REFLECTION

What is your definition of victory?

_____

_____

_____

_____

_____

_____

_____

_____

_____

_____

_____

_____

_____

_____

_____

_____

_____

_____

_____

_____

_____

_____

How will you know that you have healed from your trauma and entered into a place of great victory?

_____

_____

_____

_____

_____

_____

_____

_____

_____

_____

_____

_____

_____

_____

_____

_____

_____

_____

_____

_____

_____

_____

_____

CONCLUSION

Dr. Peter A. Levine profoundly stated, "Trauma is a fact of life. It does not, however, have to be a life sentence."[v] I am a living witness that you can bounce back after experiencing trauma. After many years of living in silence and slowly deteriorating behind the masks of the unspoken wounds and secrets of my past, I decided it was time to exchange my life sentence for early release and live a life of healing and wholeness. A life free from shame, guilt, and condemnation. A life that allows me to celebrate the survivor and overcomer that I am. A life that propels me forward to help others heal, find hope, and get the help them need to experience great victory!

Remember, healing takes time. It's a process. The journey may be uncomfortable and sometimes unbearable, but it's a journey worth taking. After trauma is healing. After healing is TRIUMPH!

Be healed. Be whole. Be well.

RESOURCES

If you or someone you know feels overwhelmed with emotions like sadness, depression, or anxiety, or want to harm themselves or others, call 911 or make contact with one of the resources below.

Mental Health Help

National Suicide Prevention Lifeline: 800-273-8255

National Domestic Violence Hotline: 800-799-SAFE (7233)

Substance Abuse and Mental Health Services Administration (SAMHSA): 800-662-HELP (4357)

Crisis Text Line: Text "MHFA" to 741741

Lifeline Crisis Chat: www.crisischat.org

Find a Therapist

www.psychologytoday.com

www.therapyforblackgirls.com

www.therapyforblackboys.com

www.openpathcollective.com

END NOTES

Introduction

i Onderko, Karen. "What Is Trauma?" Integrated Listening. Integrated Listening, October 25, 2018. https://integratedlistening.com/blog/2018/09/13/what-is-trauma/.

2. Breaking the Silence

ii "Rape." Merriam-Webster. Merriam-Webster. Accessed May 20, 2021. https://www.merriam-webster.com/dictionary/rape.

3. Behind the Mask

iii CDC Editors. "Fast Facts." Centers for Disease Control and Prevention. Centers for Disease Control and Prevention, March 23, 2021. https://www.cdc.gov/suicide/facts/index.html.

4. Let the Healing Begin

iv "Trauma Bonding: Definition, Examples, Signs, and Recovery." Medical News Today. MediLexicon International. Accessed May 21, 2021. https://www.medicalnewstoday.com/articles/trauma-bonding.

Conclusion

v Levine, Peter A., and Ann Frederick. Essay. In *Walking the Tiger Healing Trauma: the Innate Capacity to Transform Overwhelming Experiences*. Berkeley, Calif: North Atlantic Books, 1997.

ACKNOWLEDGMENTS

This book would not have been made possible without the divine plan of God. He divinely orchestrated the connections of some of the most amazing people in my life. To each of you, I am forever grateful.

First up, the one who carried me in her womb for nine months and raised me as a single mother, **Judy B. Irick**. God knew He could trust you with such a tremendous task of nurturing, protecting, and guiding me through this thing called life. For every sacrifice you made, the consistent support you give, countless prayers you render, and unconditional love you continue to show daily, I simply want to say thank you. I am honored to call you mom.

Krystal S. Irick, my beloved sister and friend, you came into this world and made mine so much better. Although I cried when I learned that I would have to share mom with you after being an only child for eighteen years, I now smile thinking of how much joy you brought to my life. You are a constant source of support and encouragement. Your future is bright. Look out world —this beauty and brain is about to take you by storm.

To my goddaughters, **Taytum, Chloe, and Morgan**, what an amazing gift each of you are to me. You are growing beautifully and I'm so proud of you. As you continue to grow and come into your own, I'll be right here cheering you on.

This healing journey is not meant to be walked alone. To my therapist, **Ms. Janice Brown**, thank you for helping me face my trauma, give language to my experiences, and ensuring that I would get to the other side victoriously. Please keep at least one appointment a month open just for me.

To my **family and friends,** you, my loves, are unmatched. I could never repay you for the genuine love and support you so effortlessly give. To those of you who believed in me, pushed me, and prayed for me to get this book project completed, thank you: Barbara Brown, DeVonya Ruffin, LaKeshia Brown, KeShawna Lampkins, Krystal Irick, Judy Irick, KeeBe Smith, Marketta Robinson, Tonya Miller, Evangela Covert, Chrislina Marshall, Raiona Denise, Wendy Buckmon, Cynthia Brown, and Sean Ledbetter.

To the entire **Brown family**, thank you for showing up for me and supporting everything I do. Your love refuels me, your prayers strengthen me, and your presence energizes me. To my **Granny**, you're no longer here, but you're forever in my heart. You are the wind beneath my wings. Your legacy lives on. I aim to make you proud. To my aunts and cousins who are in the heavenly skies with you, this one's for you, too.

A very special thank you to an incredible team of **literary professionals** who provided stellar service to help me birth my debut body of work: Brown & Brown Publishing, book cover designer, Raiona Denise, editor, Margeaux Weston of Little Blk Books, formatting by D. Ann Williams, and Author and Publishing Coach, Ayanna Williams.

Last, but certainly not least, to **every one of you** who has supported me in ministry, business, and life, thank you! To those of you who have survived traumatic experiences, your best days are ahead. Your pain is producing your purpose. Be healed, be whole, and be well so you can help others overcome, too.

STAY CONNECTED

Leave a Review

www.fromtraumatotriumphthebook.com

www.amazon.com

Social Media

Facebook & Instagram

@iamTamekaShelone

Social Media Hashtags to Use

#FromTraumaToTriumphTheBook

#TheSoulPractitionHer

Join My Mailing List

www.fromtraumatotriumphthebook.com

author@TamekaShelone.com

Learn About My Coaching Programs and Services

Subscribe to My E-mail List

www.TamekaShelone.com

ABOUT THE AUTHOR

A leader, visionary, and entrepreneur, **Tameka Shelone** serves as the Chief Executive Officer of Tameka Shelone Ministries & Enterprises, where she integrates her Christian faith with her professional coaching, counseling, and consulting services. She is a certified life coach, trained counselor, professional speaker, ordained minister, and bestselling author. As a certified trauma support specialist and mental health advocate, Tameka uses her voice to bring awareness to mental health in an effort to reduce the stigma in the African American community.

Tameka's passion and purpose are to empower, educate, and equip women to live their best lives spiritually, personally, and professionally. Through her ministry gifts of prayer, preaching, and teaching, she is fulfilling her God-given mission to spread the Gospel, share His love, and make a global impact.

Tameka's testimony of survival from relational trauma and her personal healing journey led her to discover a greater call to soul work, inner healing for women. Affectionally known as **"The Soul PractitionHer,"** Tameka equips women with the necessary tools to help them heal their M.E.S.S. (Mind, Emotions, Spirit, Soul) and break free from the emotional bondage of their past. On this journey, women find inner peace and freedom, reclaiming their lives, rediscovering their power and voice, and returning to a healthy sense of self.

Tameka is a graduate of Bowie State University with a Bachelor of Science degree in Communications and Liberty University with a Master of Arts degree in Counseling. After receiving her ministerial license in 2007, she pursued ministry training from Samuel Dewitt Proctor School of Theology.

When she's not serving in ministry and the marketplace, you can find Tameka replenishing and caring for her soul on quiet walks, journaling, connecting with nature, and traveling. Spending time with her family, sharing uncontrollable laughs and spreading unconditional love, bring her joy.

To learn more about Tameka and the services she offers, visit www.tamekashelone.com, or connect with her on Facebook or Instagram @iamtamekashelone. Be sure to subscribe to the email list and receive a free download.

To book Tameka to speak or to schedule coaching sessions, email info@tamekashelone.com.

REFLECTION

Use the next few pages as free writing. Journal any additional thoughts or feelings you may have from reading this book. Give yourself grace to feel and let your thoughts flow freely.

_____

_____

_____

_____

_____

_____

_____

_____

_____

_____

_____

_____

_____

_____

_____

_____

_____

_____

Made in the USA
Middletown, DE
09 June 2021